CH
LANES

THE MEANING TO LIFE

AND THE TRUTH ABOUT GOD

Changing Lanes: The meaning to life and the truth about God

© Jonny Pearse/Changing Lanes, 2013

Reprinted 2014 and 2018

Published by 10Publishing, a division of 10ofThose Limited.

ISBN: 9781909611054

Scripture taken from the from the NIV or ERV and indicated where appropriate.

Scripture taken from the HOLY BIBLE, NEW INTERNATIONAL VERSION®. Copyright © 1973, 1978, 1984 Biblica. Used by permission of Zondervan. All rights reserved.

The "NIV" and "New International Version" trademarks are registered in the United States Patent and Trademark Office by Biblica. Use of either trademark requires the permission of Biblica.

Easy-to-Read Version ERV, © copyright 1987, 1999, 2006 World Bible Translation Centre.

Design and Typeset by: Mike Thorpe / www.design-chapel.com

10Publishing, a division of 10ofthose.com
Unit C, Tomlinson Road, Leyland, PR25 2DY, England

Email: info@10ofthose.com

Website: www.10ofthose.com

ACKNOWLEDGEMENTS

Rachel, Sam, Claire, Emma and Lois x

MBC Youth Leaders

MBC Focus Group

Changing Lanes Supporters, Staff and Trustees

CONTENTS

BEFORE YOU START

If you've ever asked the big questions about life and God, then prepare yourself for some great answers. If you've ever thought that Christianity was just another dull religion, then you are about to be surprised. If you're looking for a new start and a different direction, then there's some good news coming your way. We're going to set out on a journey of discovery in search of the meaning to life and the truth about God. This journey could change your life forever.

Before you go any further, though, there are a few things you might find helpful.

- Think of each chapter like a jigsaw piece; the nearer you get to the end of the book, the clearer the picture should be.

- Don't worry if you haven't got a Bible; you don't *need* one to read this book. Each chapter does, however, contain some quotes from the Bible. After some of those quotes you'll notice a reference, e.g. John 14:6. The Bible is a big book, so to help us find our way around, it has been divided into separate books, chapters and verses. So for the example above the book is John, the chapter is 14 and the verse is 6. You'll get used to it.

You'll also find in each of the chapters some other small numbers; they look like this – [2]. Just ignore them, unless they really interest you. If you want to follow up any of these references, then turn to the back of the book to find out more.

If you could imagine two roads, one wide and one narrow, both going in different directions, that would be helpful. Life according to Jesus is very simple; there are just two roads in life, and two destinations after death. The first road is wide, like a motorway; there are loads of people on it but its destination is destruction. The second road is more like a narrow path; only a few people find this road but it's the only road that leads to God and eternal life. As you read each chapter, keep asking yourself the question, 'Which of the two roads am I on?'

Finally, if you are reading this as part of The Changing Lanes Course you can find more information and help on the website: www.changinglanes.org.uk

Have a great journey!

CHAPTER 1

TAKEN FOR A RIDE

WHERE BEST TO START OUR SEARCH?

If you were to set off in search of the meaning to life and the truth about God, where would you begin? If you're thinking, 'I'd start with religion', you wouldn't be the first; millions of people all over the world and all through time have headed down that same road.

It seems obvious, doesn't it? If you want to get into God then you have to get into religion. Where else would you start? Personally, I couldn't think of a worse place! Religion's so incredibly boring, it's completely confusing and way too much effort. There has to be a better way and a more exciting place to begin.

Maybe I should come clean and start by telling you what I mean by 'religion'. I mean people trying really hard to get into God's good books: obeying rules, following long lists of 'dos and don'ts' and trying to get God on their side. I'm talking about people putting in serious amounts of effort in an attempt to win God's approval. Sounds familiar? It's a bit like when you tidy your room or empty the dishwasher just before you ask your mum or dad if you can go out with your mates or invite a friend round for a sleepover. You know what I'm talking about!

WHY CAN'T WE STOP WORSHIPPING?

I've no idea why you've started to read this book or what you believe, but even if you are someone who denies the existence of God, one thing you can't deny is the existence of religion. It's a fact that wherever you go in the world, you'll always find people who worship someone or something. That's true if you climb a mountain in the Himalayas or cut your way through the deepest rainforest. Even in Britain there are people who wouldn't call themselves religious, but show all the signs that they worship the celebrities and football teams they fanatically follow. Did you know that even some atheists ('people who believe there is no god) can get religious about what they believe? Why would that be so? It's as if human beings can't help it; like it's part of who we are, of what makes us human. It seems to me that it's not a question of *if* we worship, but *what* we worship.

DID YOU KNOW THAT EVEN SOME ATHEISTS CAN GET RELIGIOUS ABOUT WHAT THEY BELIEVE?

Maybe the existence of religion is a clue or a signpost that points towards the existence of a greater being we call God. Maybe the reason we can't stop worshipping is that there is a

God who is worthy of our praise; maybe worship is something we were created to do. Surely it's a possibility worth thinking about?

WHAT'S THE PROBLEM WITH RELIGION?

If we *were* created to worship, then why isn't religion the best place for us to start our search for the meaning to life and the truth about God?

Imagine you are lost – really lost. In order for you to get back home, there are three things you'll need to know: a) where you are, b) where you are going, and c) how to get there. The big problem you'll find with so many religions is that they can't agree on a), b) or c)! They do have some things in common, but it's their differences which make religion so confusing for someone who is lost. 'God's this way,' says one religion. 'No, he's this way,' says another. Confusion can't be a great place to start.

Have you ever thought about this before: It's possible for them all to be wrong, but it's impossible for them all to be right? It's not possible for all roads to lead to God, since they are going in different directions and heading towards different destinations. Imagine if you started your big search by choosing a religion and then devoted your whole life to the wrong one. Everything you believed to be right would turn out to be wrong. Every step you took would be a step in the wrong direction. Nobody wants to be misled, so surely there's a better way and a better place to begin our search than with religion.

WHICH WAY NOW?

If there is a God, what we really need is for God to show us that He's real, and what He's like. Nobody could be more qualified to do this than God Himself. The sentence below comes from the Bible. They are the words of Jesus taken from a conversation He was having with some of His first followers (known as His disciples), and they are going to help us see something we might not have seen before.

'I AM THE WAY AND THE TRUTH AND THE LIFE. NO ONE COMES TO THE FATHER [GOD] EXCEPT THROUGH ME.'

John 14:6 (NIV)

IT'S NOT RELIGION WE NEED – IT'S REVELATION

Revelation is simply uncovering something. It's to opening something up, like unwrapping a present to see what's inside. It's what happens when a technology company launches their new product; it's a moment of revelation, unveiling what has been hidden from view. You might have been able to take a good guess at what it could be, but you wouldn't really know until it was revealed.

If we were to play a guessing game about God, I wonder what you'd imagine Him or her or it to be like. You might imagine God as an angry head teacher, or a cruel dictator, or a powerful energy force. But what are the chances of your guesses being right? I could try guessing your name, date of birth, the place you live and the hobbies you enjoy, but I'd be sure to get something wrong.

Really, what matters is not what we think about God – what matters is what's true about God. One of the reasons we have so many religions in our world could be down to people playing these kinds of guessing games for real; people saying 'I think God is like this', or 'I think God is like that'.

So, in our search for answers we need more than guessing games, and something more reliable than our ideas and imagination. We need the truth. Who better to reveal the truth about God than God? We don't need human religion – we need God's revelation. We need God to show us that He's real, and to show us what He's like. Right?

What if, at some point in human history, God stepped into our world as a human being? Imagine that! I've often asked young people what God would have to do to prove to them that He is real, and every time I get the same answer: 'Show up on earth.' Imagine not having to play guessing games any more; not needing to rely on other people's opinions. We could know for sure.

WHAT IF GOD HAS ACTUALLY, PHYSICALLY AND HISTORICALLY ALREADY SHOWN UP ON PLANET EARTH?

But what if this crazy idea about God coming to earth is not something we have to imagine? What if God has actually, physically and historically already shown up on planet Earth? What if those words we've just read from the Bible are part of an accurate historical record of the time God came to our world? What if those words are the truth about God, from God?

This is the point where you can put your imagination to one side and allow yourself to get a little bit excited. Because when we start to dig a bit deeper into the life of Jesus, that's exactly the conclusion history is leading us to believe – Jesus was God on earth.

IT'S NOT RELIGION WE NEED – IT'S RESCUE

In our search for the meaning to life and the truth about God, life can often leave us feeling quite lost. So to hear that God came to earth in person is exciting news. But what did He say? What help did He give? Which way did He point?

Imagine a group of teenagers who go on an expedition, but get completely lost and totally confused. They meet a number of people along the way who give them conflicting instructions and differing directions, so much so that the teenagers find themselves and their arguments going round in circles. To make matters worse, the sun is now setting and it is getting seriously cold. What kind of help do they need most of all? They certainly don't want or need more directions. What they need more than anything else is to be rescued.

IT MAY SURPRISE YOU TO KNOW THAT JESUS DIDN'T SPEND HIS TIME ON EARTH GIVING DIRECTIONS.

It may surprise you to know that Jesus didn't spend His time on earth giving directions. He did have many things to say, but not always what you might have expected. These are some of His words: 'I am the way and the truth and the life.

No one comes to the Father except through me.' [1] The way to God, revealed by Jesus, is not found in religion – it's found in Him. It's as if He was saying, 'I know you're lost. But you don't need to find the way to God, because the Way to God has come to find you. You don't need directions, you just need Me. You don't need to get religious about this – you need to be rescued.'

IT'S NOT RELIGION WE NEED – IT'S RELATIONSHIP

Have you ever played a 'famous faces' quiz game? How good are you at recognizing celebrity faces, even when the pictures have been distorted in some way? I guess you may know hundreds of celebrities and loads of interesting stuff about their private lives as well. But while you may know *facts* about them, you don't really know *them*. And they don't know you.

Jesus didn't appear on earth just to reveal 'facts' about God. He didn't come to tell us what we needed to know in order to pass some kind of entrance exam into heaven. Jesus' words and actions show us clearly that He wants us to experience God at a much deeper level than just knowing the 'facts'. He wants us to truly know God and to be known by God in a totally genuine, personal relationship.

If you're unsure about how true that could be, ask yourself why God would come to earth and become a human being in the first place. He can't have been here as a tourist, doing a bit of sightseeing; that's crazy. Surely God knew that the best way to relate to humans and the most effective way to communicate with them was to become one. That makes perfect sense and reveals something wonderfully exciting about this God – He's interested in us.

The God Jesus reveals in John chapter 14 is a God far beyond what anyone could imagine, a personal and intimate God, and certainly not an 'it'. Jesus said He was the Way to God, the Truth about God, and the Life from God. Wow . . . this is mind-blowing, isn't it? You couldn't make this up. We could never *fully* know a God like this, but if God came to earth we could *truly* know a God like this. [2]

Real Christianity, as found in the Bible, doesn't fit what I said about religion at the beginning of this chapter, does it? What should we call it, then, if not a religion? Well, what about 'a relationship'?

The truth about religion is that it can't help us much in our search. Its existence might show that we were made for worship, but it is of no help to us in finding our way to God.

So in our search for the meaning to life and the truth about God, it's not religion we need – it's Jesus. More about Jesus later, but as our next step let's take a look at some of the other evidence for the existence of God.

CHAPTER 2

IT'S A SIGN

WHY DOESN'T GOD SHOUT LOUDER?

Are you someone who feels there might be a God out there somewhere, but if He is, He's out of reach and out of touch? Why doesn't God make Himself a little bit clearer or shout just a little bit louder? God, for many people, is like a distant signpost; they know it's there, but can't read what it's saying. It's a little like sitting near someone who's wearing headphones. You hear music but you can't make out the song. Maybe you're thinking, 'Come on, God. Speak up, please.'

Or maybe you're one of those people who refuse to believe in God until He gives you a special sign – a supernatural encounter, or something similar. You're hoping for a message in a bottle, a light in the sky . . . even a freaky image on your cheeseburger will do! 'God, just give me a sign. Something, anything! I want to believe in You, but where's the evidence?'

MAYBE YOU'RE THINKING, 'COME ON, GOD. SPEAK UP, PLEASE.'

It's a great question to ask, and it's a question for which God has a great answer. This is what God might reply: 'The evidence is around you. It's within you and it's in front of you.'

WHERE DOES THE EVIDENCE POINT?

Don't be mistaken into thinking that scientists have got evidence and Christians have got faith. In reality, Christians look at exactly the same evidence as scientists do, but come to a different conclusion. Some of the world's greatest scientists of the past have believed in a creator God, and some of today's most brilliant scientists still do.[1]

Have you ever examined a piece of jewellery carefully? If not, ask whoever wears the most bling in your family to let you take a closer look. Good quality jewellery usually has something called a hallmark. A hallmark is like a stamp which tells you something about the material it has been made from, the date it was made, and the designer who made it. You might need a magnifying glass, but you should be able to see some symbols and maybe a code. These tiny pieces of information will tell you something very important about the origin of the piece of jewellery. Whenever we see a hallmark, we can know that it didn't come about by accident; there was thought and time, design and planning, effort and expertise put into making it. Hallmarks always tell us that there was a designer and creator involved.

SOME OF THE WORLD'S GREATEST SCIENTISTS OF THE PAST HAVE BELIEVED IN A CREATOR GOD.

The universe in which we live is full of hallmarks. They are like clues or signposts pointing away from an accident and towards an intelligent, designer-creator God. We all know that a painting has an artist, a car a manufacturer, a building an architect, and a robot an engineer. So does it really make sense to believe that this beautiful and complex universe came into being by accident?

You've probably heard it said (and you may have said it yourself) that 'science has disproved the existence of God'. That statement is unscientific, and completely untrue. There's not a single scientific test that could conclusively prove or disprove the existence of God. If anyone ever tells you that 'there is definitely no God', ask them if they know everything there is to know about everything – they don't. Even if they knew most things, what if the thing they didn't know about was God?

Science, of course, is useful in so many areas of life, but in our search for the meaning of life and the truth about God, science has its limitations. If a scientist randomly stumbled across a chocolate chip cookie, they could tell you what it was and the ingredients it was made from. They would even conclude (in this instance) that someone had made it. What they couldn't tell you, however, was *who* made it and *why*. We need the baker to step forward in order to reveal that kind of information: 'I made it. I made it for my son's lunch.' Science is helpful in examining the evidence, but there is more to this search than science. [2]

SO WHAT'S THE TRUTH ABOUT EVIDENCE?

THE HEAVENS TELL ABOUT THE GLORY OF GOD.

THE SKIES ANNOUNCE WHAT HIS HANDS HAVE MADE.

EACH NEW DAY TELLS MORE OF THE STORY,

AND EACH NIGHT REVEALS MORE AND MORE
ABOUT GOD'S POWER.

YOU CANNOT HEAR THEM SAY ANYTHING.

THEY DON'T MAKE ANY SOUND WE CAN HEAR.

BUT THEIR MESSAGE GOES THROUGHOUT THE WORLD.

Psalm 19:1–4a (ERV)

IT'S AROUND US

Have you ever looked at a star-filled sky, or seen a beautiful sunset, and been left speechless? I'm sure you know that we live in a galaxy called the Milky Way; it contains more than 200 billion stars, which sounds like a lot, until you consider that it's just one of more than 100 billion galaxies in our known universe! 'Wow!' is about all you can say to that. What if those stars had a voice of their own? I wonder what they would say to you, as you looked up at them.

The Bible says that the universe in which we live is like a giant loudspeaker, shouting out for our attention. It's like the stars do have a voice because their existence tells us something important about God. 'Look,' they say. 'Listen.' Their scale and beauty are saying something like this: 'There is a God;

the universe can't be an accident. Just think about how awesomely powerful, how creatively intelligent the maker of all this must be!' A God who put the stars into space would, without doubt, definitely be a God worth praising.

Whether you look through a telescope or a microscope, the hallmarks of design can be clearly seen. Whether it's the giant Jupiter perfectly placed to protect us from tons of space debris heading in earth's direction, or the tiny bacteria moving around with great speed using what look like carefully engineered on-board motors and propellers – they are all hallmarks of design.

To believe in a creator God is not unscientific. To believe in God is to examine the evidence, to look where it's pointing, and to listen to what it's saying.

IT'S WITHIN US

I PRAISE YOU BECAUSE YOU MADE ME
IN SUCH A WONDERFUL WAY.
Psalm 139:14a (ERV)

Do you ever find yourself asking big questions about life? 'Where did I come from? Why am I here? Where am I going?' If science has already answered these questions for us, why do we still keep asking them? You wouldn't be reading this book if you *truly* believed that science has given you all the answers.

These questions we ask, these deep longings we feel, are like hallmarks, signposts, clues within us which keep on pointing us towards God. Why do we feel guilty when we commit a wrong? Why do we feel a sense of injustice when we see a crime go unpunished? Why do we have an inbuilt desire to worship? Why do even atheists find themselves crying out to God in a crisis? Why does nothing ever satisfy for very long? Why, when you have so much, do you feel so empty?

Do you ever lie awake and think, 'If I die in my sleep, is that it'? Why, when you bring death up in conversation, does nobody want to talk about it? Why does it hurt inside when someone we love dies? According to science, we are nothing more than a collection of chemicals, which means death is nothing more than the rearranging of atoms. The death of our friends and family, then, means nothing more than the death of a flower or a fly. But we know that's not true.

The way we are, the way we think, the way we question, and the deep desires within us are all pointing us away from accidental beginnings. So, it's like human beings have a hallmark stamped firmly into their lives. Wherever we find a hallmark we can be sure that whatever it is, it's been made on purpose and for a purpose.

IT'S IN FRONT OF US

'THE SON OF MAN [JESUS] CAME TO FIND LOST PEOPLE AND SAVE THEM.'
Luke 19:10 (ERV)

Wherever you go, whatever country you are in, you will meet all kinds of people who say that God has changed their lives.

Different ages and intelligence, different personalities and cultural backgrounds, they all have one thing in common: the evidence of a changed life. You'll find people like this in your community, even in your school.

Let me tell you about Adam.[3] Aged 15, he came to one of the youth groups I run. He called himself an atheist and was very sceptical about anything to do with God. He came along looking for a good time; he certainly wasn't looking for God. We had a large and fun-filled group, and would spend part of the evening looking at the message of the Bible. Over a number of weeks, the talks that Adam heard about God began to make a massive impression on him. He found that every question he had was being answered, and every excuse he came up with was just that – an excuse. Within a few months he became convinced that God was real, that God loved him

ADAM IS JUST ONE OF THE MILLIONS OF LIVING SIGNPOSTS, POINTING US TOWARDS THE REALITY OF GOD.

and that God was interested in powerfully changing his life. Adam is just one of the millions of living signposts, pointing us towards the reality of God.

The words at the beginning of this section are found in the Bible. Jesus said them about Himself just after a dramatic, life-changing encounter with a dodgy guy called Zacchaeus, [4] who was perhaps the most unpopular man in town. But once he'd met Jesus, no one could deny the amazing change in him. It was there for all to see – real evidence of God at work in the world. How do we explain stories like this – people like Adam and Zacchaeus turning their back on what they used to believe and on the way they used to behave? It's the evidence in front of us.

The truth about evidence is that it's there; the hallmarks are around us, within us and in front of us. What can we say about this evidence? It's a sign from God pointing to God, pointing away from a Big crazy Bang and pointing towards a big Creator God.

CHAPTER 3

DODGY STEERING

WHAT'S WRONG WITH OUR WORLD?

If you were only allowed to use two words to describe our world, what would they be? The two words I'd choose would be 'beautiful' and 'broken'. Wherever I look, I see evidence of them both; sometimes they exist side by side, and sometimes on their own. Have you also noticed that beautiful things don't stay beautiful for long? Think about a once-beautiful valley now dry and deserted, a once-beautiful city now completely ruined by war, a once-beautiful child now damaged by drug abuse, or that once-beautiful family now separated by lies and deceit.

When you see on TV some of the awful things that are going on in our world, do you ever get an empty feeling deep down inside? You know there's something wrong, you sense there's something more, and you long for something better. How do you explain those deep emotions? I think the best explanation is the most obvious one: there *is* something wrong, there *is* something more, and there *is* something better.

WHO MESSED IT UP?

So, who's to blame for the way our world is today? Some people like to point the finger towards God. If He made our world to begin with, then who else is there to blame? Hang on a minute, though. Just before you start blaming God, there's something you need to consider.

If NASA[1] discovered the perfect planet, the last thing we should do is put human beings on it. Why not? Because we'd spoil it, fight over it and pollute it. How long before the first murder, or act of terrorism? Could it be true, then, that the reason there's something wrong with our world is that there's something wrong with us?

The first book of the Bible, which is called Genesis, describes a beautiful and perfect world to begin with. A loving God created a stunning world without anything spoiling it. He placed the care of His world into the hands of the first human beings. They were perfect to begin with, too, and perfectly free to make moral choices. Tragically, they didn't want to take care of God's world. They wanted to take control of it. The Genesis story tells how they rejected God as their ruler, and how God in return gave them over to what they wanted – self-rule. It was like they grabbed the steering wheel from God, chucked the maker's manual out of the window, and drove off at speed, taking the world in a whole new direction. They chose their own way, not God's way.

A LOVING GOD CREATED A STUNNING WORLD WITHOUT ANYTHING SPOILING IT.

Their choices came with terrible consequences for us and for the world; the earth was cursed, relationships broken and perfection lost. Yes, you can still see that our world was made to be beautiful, but the brokenness runs through the rest of the Genesis story. The world we see around us is not the world as God made it. It's the world as *we* have made it.

IT'S NOT MY PROBLEM, IS IT?

Instead of pointing the finger towards God, then, maybe we should be pointing the finger at the first human beings. What were they thinking of? Themselves! They had a world that we can only dream about, a world we all long for, and they messed it up for everyone. But before we get too carried away, there's something else we need to consider. Where does God fit into our lives? Where does He fit into *yours*? If God gives you your every breath, your every heartbeat, your every moment as a gift, what are you doing with the life He has given you? Who's holding the steering wheel in *your* life? Which way are you heading? Can you be sure that you would not have done the same as the first human beings, if you had been them? What they did reflects what human beings have been doing ever since – going our own way, doing our own thing, living life without God at the centre. Jesus calls that way the 'wide . . . road that leads to destruction'. [2] More about that in the next chapter.

There's a little word in the Bible which summarises our big rebellion against God; it's called 'sin'. Sin is our refusal to go God's way. Sin means we fall short of God's perfect standard.

It's like an arrow aimed at a target which not only fails to hit the bull's-eye, it drops short of the target altogether. The Bible says: 'for all have sinned and fall short of the glory of God'. [3] You might not say it quite like that, but you could say 'nobody's perfect', which is the same thing, just different words. Let's be honest. None of us, not me, not you, could be trusted with a perfect planet.

If I drew a straight line which marked God's perfect standard, how near to the line do you think the best human being could get? Not very close! Now, what about the worst person you can think of? And where would you place yourself? Somewhere in the middle, I'd guess. What do you notice? Yes, we're all the wrong side of the line. We're all in the same boat, we all have the same problem, no one's perfect, all have sinned – say it how you like, what the Bible says about us is true. What's wrong with the world? I am!

IS SIN REALLY OUR BIGGEST PROBLEM?

.. SO THEY WENT TO THE ROOF ABOVE JESUS AND MADE A HOLE IN IT. THEN THEY LOWERED THE MAT WITH THE PARALYZED MAN ON IT. WHEN JESUS SAW HOW MUCH FAITH THEY HAD, HE SAID TO THE PARALYZED MAN, 'YOUNG MAN, YOUR SINS ARE FORGIVEN. . . . MAYBE YOU ARE THINKING IT WAS EASY FOR ME TO SAY TO THE CRIPPLED MAN, "YOUR SINS ARE FORGIVEN." THERE'S NO PROOF IT REALLY HAPPENED. BUT WHAT IF I SAY TO THE MAN, "STAND

**UP. TAKE YOUR MAT AND WALK"? THEN YOU WILL
BE ABLE TO SEE IF I REALLY HAVE THIS POWER OR
NOT.' SO JESUS SAID TO THE PARALYZED MAN, 'I
TELL YOU, STAND UP. TAKE YOUR MAT AND GO HOME.'
IMMEDIATELY THE PARALYZED MAN STOOD UP ...**

Mark 2:4,5,9–12 (ERV)

News had been travelling fast that Jesus had the power to heal all kinds of illnesses and disabilities, so four friends brought a paralyzed man to Jesus on a kind of stretcher. The most shocking part of this story is not the point where they ripped a hole in someone else's roof – the shock comes when we hear what Jesus says next: 'Young man, your sins are forgiven.' What was this man's biggest problem? It was obvious, wasn't it? He couldn't move; he was paralyzed. Jesus, however, sees things differently. As far as God is concerned, there's no bigger problem than the problem of our sin. So, what's the truth about sin?

IT SPOILS

Sin has spoilt our world, that's clear for us to see. But it's what we can't see that's the real problem. What we see are the symptoms, what we can't see is the cause. The problem lies deep within every one of us. Why do we do the things we do? It's because of the way we are. It's like a bad tree producing bad fruit. Sin spoils every part of our lives – the way we think, the way we feel, the way we speak and the way we act.

It has spoilt our sense of direction; it makes us like a car with dodgy steering, or a supermarket trolley with a broken wheel. However hard we try to be good and do what's right, it keeps taking us the opposite way. Sin has even spoilt our ability to know what is right. It loves to deceive; it'll even deceive us into believing that wrong is right and right is wrong.

Sin has also spoilt our ability to please God; in fact, sin makes it *impossible* for us to please God. Even the very best thing you have ever done in your very best moment on your very best day is tainted by sin. The Bible uses a powerful picture to help us understand. It describes our very best good deeds as a dirty nappy or a used sanitary towel. Gross! Imagine presenting something like that to God. 'Here's what I'd like to offer You, God, to make up for my part in messing up this world.'

IT SEPARATES

Don't you hate it when you can't get through? When someone has switched off their phone or you've forgotten your password or lost your key? Ever felt as if there might be something blocking the way between you and God, a kind of roadblock stopping you going any further? There is.

One of the things sin blocks is any possibility of us enjoying a close relationship with God. The reason is that God hates sin more than anything else; He's completely sinless, perfect in every way. He literally can't stand sin. If one of your friends deliberately damages your property, or takes something valuable which belongs to you and wrecks it, what then? What would that do for your friendship? It would be impossible to pretend it didn't happen. I doubt if you'd be inviting them round for a sleepover. What they did, and what they are like, blocks the possibility of you being good friends with them; there's something getting in the way, now. Similarly our sin gets in the way and causes a relationship breakdown with God.

GOD HAS GOOD REASON TO HATE SIN – LOOK AT WHAT IT'S DONE TO HIS WORLD.

God has good reason to hate sin – look at what it's done to His world. The reason for this, is that God hates sin more than anything else; it blocks us from being the people He made us to be. Sin stops us from getting the most out of our lives and restricts us from reaching our true potential. Sin separates. It's no wonder God can't stand sin.

IT'S SERIOUS

There are many reasons why we could class sin as serious, but perhaps what makes it so serious is the fact that we can't control it or cure it.

Many people and organizations have tried to fix our world; it's great that people care enough to try, but so often they attack the symptoms and not the cause. That's like pushing a broken-down car to the carwash. You can make it look cleaner on the outside, but the problem is under the bonnet. Spraying deodorant on a dead body might make the air smell fresher, but it's not going to bring the corpse back to life. Now, this is getting seriously depressing. But I've been saving the good news for the end! Let's go back to the story of the paralyzed man, because it's there that we can see just how serious God is about a solution for the problem.

In the same way that only you can forgive your friend for wrecking your stuff, it's only God who can forgive us for messing up His world. By forgiving and healing the man, Jesus was showing us that He is willing and able to forgive sin. The message is clear; God's solution to our sin can only be found in Jesus.

So the story wasn't only good news for the man on the mat; it's great news for us. There are two things we need for the problem of our sin: forgiveness from God, and the power to get up and live a new life – the very things Jesus came to earth to give to us.

CHAPTER 4

COLLISION COURSE

WE ALL BELIEVE IN JUSTICE, DON'T WE?

Violent rape, murder, hit-and-run, child abuse or news of a shocking crime in your street would certainly get the neighbours talking, but what if you came home to find that some of those crimes had been committed against the people you love the most? How would you feel about that? It would be pretty weird if you just shrugged your shoulders and said you didn't care, that it didn't matter. I'm guessing you'd feel angry; you'd demand that whoever did this must be caught and punished. We all believe in justice, don't we? So does God. Wouldn't it be terrible if God just shrugged His shoulders or turned a blind eye to all the wrongs and injustices in our world? The Bible from beginning to end reveals a God who cares enough to be angry at everything that is wrong, and who is serious enough to always demand justice, if not in this life then in the life to come.

But while we all believe in justice, the trouble is, when it comes to sin we're all guilty. Ouch! If God has prepared a place of punishment for the guilty, then let's face it, that's where we're heading. According to Jesus, a place of punishment for sin already exists; it's the place we call hell.

WHY TAKE HELL SO SERIOUSLY?

Jesus' teaching about hell is unavoidable. If you want to go on holiday to France, you can't avoid the fact that there is a channel of water separating our two countries. You could airbrush it off the road atlas, you could refuse to ever speak about it, even believe with all your heart that it isn't there, but the unavoidable reality remains the same. You have to go under it, fly over it or sail on it. So, what do we do with the teaching of Jesus about hell? You could airbrush it out of your copy of the Bible, never speak about it again, or even believe with all your heart that Jesus didn't ever mention the place. But the reality doesn't change; it's unavoidable.

We're not going to pretend; we're going to take it seriously and hit head-on what Jesus had to say about it. Before we do that, however, let's just ask why we should trust Jesus on this one. You will have already heard many differing views about life after death. The question is, whom should you trust? What do *you* believe will happen to you when you die? Who told you that? How do *they* know what they have told you is true? Is there a possibility they could be wrong?

In the Bible there are four books called Gospels (gospel means 'good news'). They each tell the historical story of the life of Jesus; they contain a record of His actions and His words. If you read one or even all of these Gospels, you'll notice straight away just how powerful the words of Jesus were. He certainly wasn't all talk; his actions spoke as loud as His words. When He addressed the evil spirits, they trembled; when He taught the crowds, they were amazed. When He said to a paralyzed man, 'get up' [1], he did; when He commanded a storm to 'Be still' [2], it was; when He told a dead girl to 'wake up' [3], she came to life; and when He spoke about the future, His words came true. [4] His record speaks for itself. Now, place Jesus alongside the person who taught you about life after death; how do they compare? Who is the most qualified and reliable?

Fire alarms in school can be a welcome break from lessons, but if the alarm always turns out to be false, then after a while the pupils and teachers learn to ignore them. It reaches the point where nobody trusts the warning sound; its history says the alarm's not worth trusting. Jesus' track record, however, is completely reliable; the gospel stories should fill us with confidence and trust. His words were always loving, powerful and true; so it's sensible to listen carefully and take seriously His warnings about hell.

WHERE'S THE EXIT?

'ENTER THROUGH THE NARROW GATE. FOR WIDE IS THE GATE AND BROAD IS THE ROAD THAT LEADS TO DESTRUCTION, AND MANY ENTER THROUGH IT. BUT SMALL IS THE GATE AND NARROW THE ROAD THAT LEADS TO LIFE, AND ONLY A FEW FIND IT.'
Matthew 7:13,14 (NIV)

Two gates, two roads and two destinations. This is how Jesus wants us to picture the reality of this life and the life to come. The picture is not a difficult one to understand, the maths is easy; there isn't a third option. Option one is the wide road, leading away from God and heading towards a place called hell. Option two is the narrow road, leading to God and heading towards paradise, a place we call heaven. That's the truth about hell according to Jesus:

IT'S AWFUL

It was 'a hell of a goal', 'a hell of a party', 'a hell of a pizza'. Everyday phrases which sadly disguise the awfulness of hell as described by Jesus. Don't be fooled into believing that if there is a hell then it's a fun-filled, heavy metal party from the set of a music video. Jesus tells it quite differently. According to Him, it's a real place – definitely not a myth or a metaphor. It was originally created by God as a place of lasting punishment for the devil and his fallen angels. The way in which Jesus describes it should fill us with quiet awe. Please don't take my word for it. Take some time out today and read for yourself. [5]

DON'T BE FOOLED INTO BELIEVING THAT IF THERE IS A HELL THEN IT'S A FUN-FILLED, HEAVY METAL PARTY.

Jesus called hell by a number of different names, and described it in a number of different ways. One of the names was 'Gehenna'. [6] Outside the city of Jerusalem during the time Jesus lived was a rubbish tip with a horrible history; it was called Gehenna. It's was Jerusalem's dumping ground; it was where they would throw rubbish, sewage and even dead bodies.

The slow-burning fire of Gehenna never went out; day and night it would burn, and the maggots there never stopped moving. The sight and the smell must have been unbearable. Gehenna was to be avoided at all costs. The fact that it was outside of the city wall gives us a powerful and helpful contrast. Inside the city there was life, love and care, safety and security, fun and family, singing and dancing, food and laughter, pleasure and joy. Life in the city was a completely different world to Gehenna; the city was paradise in comparison.

Do you see the picture Jesus was painting? To be in hell is to be cut off and locked out of a wonderful life to come; truly awful.

IT'S AWAITING

We can't avoid the fact that Jesus had much to say about hell, and we can't avoid the fact that what He did say sounds awful. Perhaps most shocking of all is the realization that 'You don't have to take a wrong turn to find yourself on the wide road that leads to hell. You're already on it!'

To help us understand this, we need to go back to the Genesis story for a moment. Remember that the wrong turn was taken back in the beginning. Humanity has been on the wide road ever since; that's the reality Jesus wants us to be aware of. Jesus also wants us to know what it is that lies at the end of that road. Sin not only separates from God in this life but it sets us on course for hell in the life to come; it's awaiting. We are on a collision course.

Have you ever seen those huge, flashing, warning signs on the motorway? 'FOG', 'ACCIDENT AHEAD', 'SLOW' and so on. So depressing, so inconvenient. It's not the news you *wanted* to hear on your journey, but certainly the news you *needed* to hear; your life could depend on how seriously you take those warnings. God cares enough about sin to punish it. That's good. He also cares enough about sinful people to send His Son, Jesus, into the world to warn us of the danger we're in. That's amazing! If we could make the teaching of Jesus about hell into a road sign, it would say something like 'Danger ahead, take the next exit'.

IT'S AVOIDABLE

Since Jesus warns us so clearly about the dangers of hell, we can be sure of two very important facts – first, that God doesn't want us to go there, and secondly that there must be a way of escape; there must be an exit.

In order for us to see this demonstrated in practice, let's zoom in for a moment to the point in history where Jesus dies. Though Jesus had done nothing deserving of death, He was framed by the religious leaders and then executed by Roman soldiers on a wooden cross between two guilty criminals. Guess where the execution took place? Outside the city of Jerusalem near that place called Gehenna. The criminals on either side of Jesus had lived their lives in the fast lane and they were now moments from meeting their ultimate destination – hell. Listen to one of the criminals as he tells the other one to shut up, and then turns to Jesus with a request:

'YOU SHOULD FEAR GOD. ALL OF US WILL DIE SOON. YOU AND I ARE GUILTY. WE DESERVE TO DIE BECAUSE WE DID WRONG. BUT THIS MAN HAS DONE NOTHING WRONG.' THEN HE SAID, 'JESUS, REMEMBER ME WHEN YOU BEGIN RULING AS KING!' THEN JESUS SAID TO HIM, 'I PROMISE YOU, TODAY YOU WILL BE WITH ME IN PARADISE.'

Luke 23:40–43 (ERV)

Moments from death he admits his guilt and literally turns to Jesus, believing that He had the willingness to forgive his sin, the power to save him from hell, and the authority to assure him of a place in paradise. Please don't think that paradise is sitting on a cloud for eternity, playing a harp; that sounds more like hell to me than heaven. When Jesus speaks of paradise we need to think in terms of a perfect life to come – remember the contrast of life inside and outside of the

PLEASE DON'T THINK THAT PARADISE IS SITTING ON A CLOUD FOR ETERNITY, PLAYING A HARP.

city. Think of paradise as a return to the perfect world we lost in the Genesis story, only this time we won't mess it up.

What's clear from this story is that Jesus not only came to

warn us about the reality of hell, He came to save us from it. It's avoidable. We'll look at how all that works in chapter 6 but for now just keep in mind that Jesus took the punishment so that we won't have to.

YES, GOD LOVED THE WORLD SO MUCH THAT HE GAVE HIS ONLY SON, SO THAT EVERYONE WHO BELIEVES IN HIM WOULD NOT BE LOST BUT HAVE ETERNAL LIFE.

John 3:16 (ERV)

There are many things you can afford to get wrong during this life on earth; this is not one of them. The first criminal gets hell, the other gets heaven. What's the one thing that made all the difference? He turned to Jesus.

CHAPTER 5

HITTING THE BRAKES

FLUKE, FAKE OR FACT?

A group of walkers stumbled across some pottery on farmland and called in a team of specialist archaeologists. During the dig, they unearth some old coins and a broken pot containing an ancient scroll. The treasure was dated and found to be almost a thousand years old. The team were surprised that the writing on the scroll had survived for so long, but the biggest surprise came when they realized what the scroll actually said. It was all about *you*. It stated your name, your date and place of birth, members of your family tree and loads of other specific facts about your life, all of which were completely true.

OK, I made the story up. But imagine something like that happening to you. Apart from completely freaking you out, what would you make of it? And what do you think people would make of you?

If all we had was history to prove that Jesus was somebody very special that would be enough. But it's not all we have.

There's something more. It's called prophecy (stating the future before it has happened).

The Bible contains sixty-six books in total, written over a period of 1,500 years. It's split into two main sections, the Old Testament and the New Testament. The Old was written before Jesus was born, and the New was written afterwards. The Old Testament contains many detailed and specific prophecies about the birth, life and death of Jesus. These prophecies were written and published hundreds of years before His birth.

One prophecy names Bethlehem as the place He would be born;[1] another describes, in detail, His death by crucifixion[2] (being nailed to a cross and left to die), long before Roman crucifixion had been invented. What do you make of that? These prophecies were so specific and numerous we can't put them down to a fluke, and they're definitely not something that could be faked. But that leaves only one possible explanation – supernatural fact. Whoever fulfilled these supernatural prophecies had to be someone super-special.

WHOEVER FULFILLED THESE SUPERNATURAL PROPHECIES HAD TO BE SOMEONE SUPER-SPECIAL.

WHICH ONE IS JESUS?

Let's say that you lived about two thousand years ago, around the time Jesus did. If you'd never met Jesus before, you might have walked right past Him in the street and never known. Jesus looked completely ordinary. There wasn't a halo around His head like you see on the Christmas cards; there wasn't any spooky choir music accompanying everything He said, like you hear in the movies. If you'd seen Jesus standing next to one of his first followers (they were called disciples), you might have asked, 'Which one is Jesus?'

So, if all you had to go on was His outward appearance, then you'd be less than impressed. But it wasn't what He looked like that made Him so special. It's what He *said* and *did* which set Him apart from the crowd.

Aged just 12 He was astounding some of the brightest minds in the land with His knowledge and understanding.[3] When an adult, the crowds who followed Him were totally amazed[4] and His enemies who questioned Him were thoroughly slammed.[5] His words carried a power and authority not heard of before – everyone was talking about Him[6]

With His words He healed the blind,[7] and the deaf[8] and the lame.[9] You already know about the paralyzed man on a mat. Once He healed a man who was in a different location,[10] and then there was the bleeding woman who was healed by just touching the edge of His cloak.[11] There were at least three separate occasions when Jesus brought dead people back to life again. There was a sick girl who had just died at home, a young man in the middle of his own funeral, and on another occasion a man called Lazarus who had been dead and buried a few days.[12] You don't need me to point it out, but ordinary people can't do this kind of thing.

Please don't think that these miracles can be explained away as myths or exaggerated stories. It's important to note that the miracles Jesus performed were nearly always in public. If someone told me that they had performed a miracle, the first thing I'd want to know would be, 'Did anybody else see it? Were there any witnesses?' When Jesus changed water into wine,[13] He wasn't at home, He was at a wedding; that makes a massive difference.

You also need to factor in that when the writers of the Gospels published these stories, it was within the lifetime of the people who were there. If these stories were made up or exaggerated, then these Gospels would not have been accepted as true in the first place and couldn't have stood the test of time.[14]

WHO IS THIS?

A FURIOUS SQUALL CAME UP, AND THE WAVES BROKE OVER THE BOAT, SO THAT IT WAS NEARLY SWAMPED. JESUS WAS IN THE STERN, SLEEPING ON A CUSHION. THE DISCIPLES WOKE HIM AND SAID TO HIM, 'TEACHER, DON'T YOU CARE IF WE DROWN?' HE GOT UP, REBUKED THE WIND AND SAID TO THE WAVES, 'QUIET! BE STILL!' THEN THE WIND DIED DOWN AND IT WAS COMPLETELY CALM. HE SAID TO HIS DISCIPLES, 'WHY ARE YOU SO AFRAID? DO YOU STILL HAVE NO FAITH?' THEY WERE TERRIFIED AND ASKED EACH OTHER, 'WHO IS THIS? EVEN THE WIND AND THE WAVES OBEY HIM!'

Mark 4:37–41 (NIV)

One minute Jesus is asleep in the back of a boat, the next He is speaking to a raging storm and it becomes completely calm. Sleeping like a human being, then speaking with the power of God. Ordinary, but extraordinary! No wonder people were asking the question, 'Who is this man called Jesus?' So, what is the truth about Him?

IT'S HISTORICAL

The great thing about the story of Jesus is that it's not just a great story, it's a great story set in history. History is not like philosophy; it can be investigated in a specific way, records can be checked, dates can be cross-referenced, locations examined and sites excavated. Whenever a historical document mentions names, dates and places (which the Gospels do) – they can be checked. Did you know that there are thousands of old, very old and ancient copies of New Testament documents in existence? You might not find that exciting, but it's the kind of thing historians go crazy about. Jesus lifts the God question off the pages of philosophy and plants it onto the pages of history – that's really significant.

THE GREAT THING ABOUT THE STORY OF JESUS IS THAT IT'S... A GREAT STORY SET IN HISTORY.

You'd expect, wouldn't you, if someone as amazing as Jesus had walked on planet Earth that there would be other records too? Not just the Bible? Surely other historians would have mentioned Him as well? They have! In fact, two famous historians – one was Jewish [15] and the other

Roman [16] – both mention Jesus by name, and make a reference to His miracles. So, when you start to put the historical jigsaw pieces together, an interesting picture starts to appear. Jesus Christ really was a historical character, and all the evidence points to Him being somebody very special.

Imagine the prime minister suggesting that the world should set the calendar to zero as from now. All of time in the past, present and future should now centre around this new date. Not likely! Something extraordinary would have to happen in the history of the world for us to even think about such a crazy idea as that. Maybe something as significant as God showing up on earth . . .? I know Jesus divides opinion, but He's the only man who divides history – that has to tell you something.

I KNOW JESUS DIVIDES OPINION, BUT HE'S THE ONLY MAN WHO DIVIDES HISTORY.

IT'S RADICAL

There are loads of reasons why I believe the story of Jesus is true, but one reason that you may not have considered before is this: it's just so radically different from anything else. Think about it. It's not something you'd make up. Who could have thought of something like this? Who would invent a story that involves the God who made the universe and everything in it coming to earth as a baby, being born in a stable, then learning to walk and talk, growing up to be a man, and dying on a cross to make it possible for sinners to get to heaven?

That's so radically different from what usual 'religion' says! Religion says, 'These are the steps you need to take to get to God.' Jesus says, 'God has stepped down to earth.' Religion says, 'This is what you must do to be saved.' Jesus says, 'This is what God has done to save you.' Religion says, 'This way to God.' Jesus says, 'I am the Way.' You may not have seen it before, but there's a radical point of difference between true Christianity and the other religions of this world – if we were to sum up the message of Christianity in a sentence, it would be something like this: 'It's good news *from* God *about* Jesus *for* everyone who will believe.' That's way too radical for it to be made up, even for the most intelligent or imaginative mind.

IT'S LOGICAL

If a new kid started in your class and you introduced yourself and he smiled back and said, 'Hi, I'm God', you'd laugh in his face. You might even want to punch him in the face! Would it surprise you to know that these kinds of claims have actually happened? Yes, history records from time to time that ordinary people have claimed to be God. So, back to that new weird kid in your class. Is he God, or not? Is his claim true, or is it false? What does the evidence say? What's the logical conclusion? These are the same questions we need to apply to Jesus. What does the evidence say? What's the logical conclusion? There are three possible explanations for you to consider about Jesus. Was He mad? Was He was bad? Or was He God? [17]

By mad I mean out of His mind; seriously mentally

disturbed. By bad I mean in His right mind, but some kind of evil trickster; a lying, deceiving cheat. By God I mean the greatest being there is, the all-powerful Creator. One of these three explanations has to fit. So, ask yourself, where does the evidence point? His words and His works, the miracles, the eyewitnesses, the written records, the fulfilled prophecy – what's the logical conclusion? Mad? Not according to the evidence. Bad? No, definitely not; you'll find His words were genuine and His actions were selfless.[18] Right – let's hit the brakes, let's stop for a moment and think this through. If He wasn't mad and He wasn't bad then logically He must be God. There's no other option.

When Jesus was in the storm-tossed boat, He turned to the disciples just after He had calmed the storm and asked them a searching question: 'Do you still have no faith?'[19] He'd already given them more than enough evidence for them to believe what was true about His identity – He really was God on earth. The evidence was there; they were just slow in believing what should have been obvious.

Let me ask you the question Jesus asked His disciples. Do you still have no faith? Faith isn't believing in something that isn't real; that's stupidity. Faith isn't a leap in the dark; that's dangerous. Faith isn't hoping for a good result; that's gambling. True faith simply believes in what is true. This story about Jesus is historical, radical and logical. And the most amazing thing about His story is: IT'S TRUE!

CHAPTER 6

GREEN LIGHT TO GOD

WHAT ON EARTH WAS GOD DOING?

If Jesus was God on earth, there's a very important and obvious question we now need to ask: what on earth was God doing? We've seen Jesus revealing, teaching and healing, but was that it? Was there a bigger plan and a greater mission?

Imagine you see a road traffic accident. A car with four lads in it spins out of control and bursts into flames. Other people start shouting advice: 'Turn off the engine'; 'Climb through the sunroof'; 'Smash the window'; 'Use your fire extinguisher'. But what do the guys in the car need more than anything else? They need to be rescued. They need someone willing to risk their life so that they can be saved from the danger they are in.

WE'VE SEEN JESUS REVEALING, TEACHING AND HEALING, BUT WAS THAT IT?

Do you know what the name Jesus means? When you know what His name means, you'll begin to understand 'what on earth He was doing'. His name means 'Saviour',[1] or we could understand it to mean 'God to the rescue'; His name tells us exactly what He came to do. Jesus was not only God on earth, He was God on a mission – a daring mission to save His people from their sins.

WASN'T THERE ANOTHER WAY?

As you've been reading this book and learning about the life and death of Jesus, have you ever asked *why* Jesus allowed Himself to be executed? It's an important question. If He had the power to heal the sick, calm the storm and raise the dead, then surely He was powerful enough to resist arrest, and smart enough to defend Himself in court. Why didn't He? Why didn't He fight for His rights? It's not difficult to see He was innocent; He'd done nothing deserving of death. Even the judge at His trial said, 'I find no fault in Him.'[2] Crucifixion was the most barbaric method of execution known, used by the Romans for the most heinous crimes. They pinned a statement of those crimes to the cross to warn onlookers against similar behaviour. But the notice above the head of Jesus just said, 'The King of the Jews'.[3] There was nothing bad to say; they couldn't pin any crimes on Jesus. So, the question remains – if He was powerful and innocent, why did Jesus allow Himself to be killed?

IF HE WAS POWERFUL AND INNOCENT, WHY DID JESUS ALLOW HIMSELF TO BE KILLED?

To understand all of this we need to understand that Jesus'

death was not a tragic accident, it wasn't just a terrible miscarriage of justice, or a bit of bad luck; it was, in fact, all part of God's amazing rescue plan for sinners – Jesus *had* to die to sort out the problem of our sin.

There's a verse in the Bible which will help us to realize why Jesus *had* to die; it will help us to see that His death was the only way for our sin-debt to be paid. The verse says 'For the wages of sin is death, but the gift of God is eternal life in Christ Jesus our Lord.' [4] If the wages (the payment, or punishment) for sinning against God is death and hell, and we're incapable of dealing with it ourselves, then our greatest need is to find someone willing to pay our sin-debt for us. Of course, it needs to be someone who doesn't have a sin-debt of their own, which limits the options to just one – Jesus! Thankfully Jesus steps in and says, 'I'll pay. I'll put things straight between you and God the Father [5] by paying your sin-debt for you. The payment is death, and I'm willing to die in your place.'

In your search for the meaning of life and the truth about God, could you ever have imagined a God like this? A God who loves sinners so much that He'd willingly step into their shoes and die for them? Jesus didn't come to earth only to give us direction, opinions or advice; He came to rescue us – that was always the plan. If someone was to pick up one of the Gospels and read the life story of Jesus for the first time, then Jesus' death should not come as a surprise to the reader; He hadn't kept his rescue mission a secret. In fact, He kept on saying that he *must* be killed; [6] there wasn't another option.

Ever wondered why Christians *celebrate* the death of Jesus? Ever wondered why they call the day Jesus died *Good* Friday? Ever wondered why Christians are always talking about the cross, and why they wear it as a badge or a piece of jewellery? It's kind of weird when you think about it, especially when you consider that the cross was designed to torture and kill people. You'll only begin to understand how special the cross is to a Christian when you realize that it was the place where Jesus paid the price for their sin.

HOW DO WE KNOW IT WORKED?

AT NOON THE WHOLE COUNTRY BECAME DARK. THIS DARKNESS CONTINUED UNTIL THREE O'CLOCK. AT THREE O'CLOCK JESUS CRIED OUT LOUDLY, 'ELOI, ELOI, LAMA SABACHTHANI.' THIS MEANS 'MY GOD, MY GOD, WHY HAVE YOU LEFT ME ALONE?' . . . THEN JESUS CRIED OUT LOUDLY AND DIED. WHEN JESUS DIED, THE CURTAIN IN THE TEMPLE WAS TORN INTO TWO PIECES. THE TEAR STARTED AT THE TOP AND TORE ALL THE WAY TO THE BOTTOM.
Mark 15:33,34,37,38 (ERV)

If Jesus' death was payment for our sin-debt, how do we know it worked? How can we be sure that God the Father accepted the payment? How can we be sure right now that God is willing to forgive *our* sin and cancel *our* debt? Let me explain. Here's the truth about forgiveness:

IT'S COSTLY

Let's travel back to the day Jesus died. Jesus was dying. He'd been beaten to the point that He could hardly be recognized. People had spat on Him, punched Him and ripped the hair out of His beard. The soldiers had pushed a crown of sharp thorns onto His head and forced Him to carry a heavy wooden cross, which they nailed Him to. Then at midday it went dark – a scary darkness covered the land; Jesus could no longer be seen clearly. This wasn't an eclipse; it was the wrong time of year for that, and no eclipse has ever lasted for three hours. This was a supernatural darkness sent by God the Father – it was a sign, but what was it saying? Darkness in the Bible is sometimes connected with God's anger against sin, but if so, then who at this point in the story was God the Father angry with?

Maybe He was angry with the religious leaders for setting Jesus up,[7] or maybe with the crowd for getting behind the religious leaders and shouting 'Crucify him!'.[8] Maybe God was angry with Judas, the disciple who betrayed Jesus[9],

JESUS CRIES OUT, 'MY GOD MY GOD WHY HAVE YOU FORSAKEN ME?'

or maybe with the other disciples for running away from Him.[10] Maybe God was angry with the judge who sentenced Jesus to death[11], or maybe with the Roman soldiers for mocking and beating Him before nailing Him to the cross.[12] Maybe; but from what Jesus says in the moments before He dies, we can be sure that God the Father was angry with – Jesus!

Jesus cries out, 'My God my God why have you forsaken [abandoned, left] me?' [13] God the Father seems to be treating Jesus as though He were the worst of sinners. Why would He abandon Jesus? Something must have happened in the darkness that changed the way God the Father now saw His Son. The Bible tells us that God had put onto Jesus the sins of the world; [14] God had transferred the sin of the world onto the sinless Jesus. Think of it like an online banking transaction; money going from one account to another. God had put our sin-debt into the account of Jesus, and Jesus agreed to it. For that moment in history God the Father, who can't look on sin, saw our sin on His Son. So he had to turn His back on Jesus; Jesus had to die!

GOD HAD PUT OUR SIN-DEBT INTO THE ACCOUNT OF JESUS, AND JESUS AGREED TO IT.

I think we need to pause. What does all this tell us about God's LOVE for sinners? It tells us that He was willing to do whatever it would take to forgive us, so we could be friends with Him. Jesus paid the ultimate cost, so that we don't have to. The Father had the pain of seeing His beloved Son die in agony – and have to turn His back on Him. This is breathtakingly brilliant but completely humbling. God loves YOU that much! Just shut your eyes for a moment and try to take that in.

IT'S FREE

There are many places where we are not free to enter. We can't just walk into the bank and take a look around the safe, or go into a high security prison and check out the cells. If we want to go to a theme park or concert, we need a ticket or to pay at the gate. It's not free to enter.

In the city of Jerusalem there was a temple. It was where the Jews worshipped God. Inside the Temple was a very special area called 'the Most Holy Place' – people were not free to go in there. The Most Holy Place was separated from the rest of the Temple by a huge curtain. It was more like a wall – thick and high. It was like a big 'no entry' sign or a red light that said, 'Stop. Don't go any further.' On one side sinful people, and on the other side, the presence of God. Then at the moment Jesus died, this curtain in the Temple was torn in two from top to bottom without anyone touching it! This may not sound like a big deal to you, but to the people in Jerusalem at the time, it would have been headline news.

God the Father was showing us that Jesus' death had now made a way for sinners to come into His presence. The way was now open for sinners to come to God and receive His forgiveness. There's now free entry. There's nothing for us to pay; it's been paid for in full by Jesus. In fact, just before He died, He cried out in a loud voice and said, 'It is finished', [15] which could be understood to mean 'It's been paid for'. The torn curtain was no longer like a 'no entry' sign; it was more like a green light – God showing us that there's now nothing to stop us from coming to Him for the forgiveness we so desperately need to begin a brilliant new relationship with Him.

There's a word in the Bible which is used to describe all of this. It's the word 'grace'. It simply means 'undeserved free gift'. The verse that says 'For the wages of sin is death' is a verse of two halves. It goes on to say 'but the *gift* of God is eternal life in Christ Jesus our Lord'. [16] Grace is God's free gift to the undeserving; it's a gift which gives you the opposite of what you deserve, and it's a gift that God offers to the best and worst of sinners, free of charge.

IT'S FOR YOU

If we imagined God's grace to be a gift-wrapped present, then what would be inside? Well, first you would receive forgiveness from all your sin. There would be a brand new start, and the power to take a completely different direction in your life. It would include rescue from hell, adoption into God's family, and a guaranteed place in the paradise world to come. All of which sounds great, but there's just one problem – God's grace isn't a gift-wrapped present we can see with our eyes and take up with our hands. So, how can we receive God's gift of grace? Every gift needs to be received, so how do we receive this one?

You'll need to cast your mind back to the story of the four friends who brought the paralyzed man to Jesus; can you remember what Jesus saw just before He forgave him of his sin? He saw their faith. They believed that Jesus had the power to change this man's life, so they acted on what they believed to be true. That's faith. And that's just how we're to respond and receive God's free gift of grace.

Ask yourself this. What if the four friends had stayed at

home that day and not bothered to take the man to Jesus? The answer is obvious; his life and destiny would never have changed; there would have been no healing and no forgiveness. Real faith must include real action – the only way to receive what God offers you is to respond with faith. So how do you do that?

RESPONDING WITH FAITH

Faith is simply believing what God has said and getting on with it.

> **FOR GOD SO LOVED THE WORLD THAT HE GAVE HIS ONLY BEGOTTEN [THIS MEANS: ONE AND ONLY] SON, THAT WHOEVER BELIEVES [HAS FAITH] IN HIM SHALL NOT PERISH BUT HAVE ETERNAL LIFE.**
> John 3:16 (NIV)

If you want to take God up on what He has said and accept what He is offering you, then what you are about to read will help you put your faith in Jesus.

ADMIT

There's something to Admit – that you are a sinner and in need of God's forgiveness. We've all said and done things to hurt and offend God and others. We're not perfect. We all get it wrong. Admitting that can be difficult, but it's really important.

BELIEVE

There's something to Believe – that only Jesus, through His death on the cross, can save you from your sin. You need to believe that He died in your place.

CONSIDER

There's something to Consider – two things, in fact. First, you need to consider the cost of responding with faith. Although God has promised to give you all the help you need to live your new life, it's not going to be easy. There will be some tough decisions to take and some big changes to make in your life. Secondly, you need to consider the cost of not responding with faith. Consider what it will mean to reject God's offer of forgiveness.

DO

There's something to Do – it's time for action. What you need to do is to turn away from the life you have been living and turn to God. You can do that right now by praying this prayer:

DEAR GOD, I'M SO SORRY THAT I'VE BEEN GOING MY OWN WAY UP UNTIL NOW. SORRY FOR PUSHING YOU OUT OF MY LIFE. I KNOW I NEED TO CHANGE LANES AND GET OFF THIS WIDE ROAD THAT LEADS TO DESTRUCTION. THANK YOU FOR SENDING JESUS TO DIE IN MY PLACE, AND FOR PAYING THE PRICE MY SIN

DESERVES. PLEASE FORGIVE ME. I WANT TO ACCEPT THAT AMAZING FREE GIFT YOU ARE OFFERING ME, SO I'M READY RIGHT NOW TO TURN AWAY FROM MY SIN AND TURN TO JESUS FOR MY NEW LIFE AND MY NEW START. THANK YOU, GOD!

Why not write down the time and the date and your thoughts:

_____

_____

_____

_____

_____

_____

_____

_____

_____

_____

It's also quite important to tell someone what you have done. If you have Christian friends or a youth leader you trust – or the person who gave you this book – tell them that you have said this prayer.

CHAPTER 7

INTO GEAR

WHICH WAY NEXT?

If somebody told me there were little green aliens living on Mars, I'd try to keep a straight face and probably say, 'Are you sure?' It's not very believable, is it? So, how would you react if I told you that after Jesus had been executed and buried in a tomb (a hole cut in rock) He actually, physically rose from the dead? How believable is that?

Imagine what it must have felt like being one of Jesus' disciples just after He had been killed; they must have been devastated. Their world had just been turned upside down; the person they had left everything for was dead. All their hopes and dreams must have died with Jesus. They did what I think you or I would have done – they went into hiding. [1] Perhaps they thought that they might be next. They were fearful and powerless. The power that had been driving their lives for the past few years was dead and buried. It looked as if they were going to have to roll back home to their old jobs and old way of life.

Now, if I told you that just a few weeks later, the disciples were no longer in hiding and they were not back at home, where do you think they might be? What do you think they would be doing? Would you believe me if I told you that they were now confidently and bravely telling thousands of people about Jesus and His power to change lives? Wow, what a turnaround that would be! The book of the Bible called Acts (Actions) tells exactly that story. The question is: How do you explain such a transformation in the disciples? How could such ordinary people change so much and then go on to change the world? There's only one explanation that could possibly make any sense – Jesus really did rise from the dead.

WHERE'S THE PROOF?

Did you know that there's so much evidence to show that Jesus was alive after His death that some people have said that He didn't really die? Let's take a look to see what the evidence says. [2]

To believe that Jesus didn't die is to believe that the Roman soldiers didn't do their job properly. We do know that Jesus was killed by experts; Roman soldiers were well trained and good at what they did. Failure to kill a prisoner who'd been sentenced to death under the authority of Rome would probably have cost them their own lives. We need to remember too that the soldiers didn't work alone; they were also supervised by a centurion boss, who pronounced Jesus dead at the scene. Oh, and to make sure, one of the soldiers rammed a spear through Jesus' side; eyewitnesses saw blood and water gush out of that wound. [3] That should do it!

OK, the evidence is pretty clear, but could there be another explanation? Something like, the reason that Jesus' tomb was empty was that the people who found it went to the wrong one? I guess it's worth asking that question, but there are three good reasons to say they got the right one. First, the tomb was private; it belonged to a well-known person in the community. [4] Secondly, the women who were first to find the empty tomb had already watched Jesus being put in *that* tomb, [5] and thirdly, if they got it wrong, then so did the angel [6] who met them there. It's difficult to believe that anyone got the wrong address, which means that the most obvious explanation of it being empty was that Jesus was no longer there.

OK, THE EVIDENCE IS PRETTY CLEAR, BUT COULD THERE BE ANOTHER EXPLANATION?

What if the reason it was empty was that the disciples had stolen the body? Sounds plausible, until you factor in two important details; the tomb was blocked by a massive stone, [7] possibly weighing more than 1,000 k.g., and then it was protected by an armed guard. [8] Who moved the stone? Who overpowered the guards? It can't have been the disciples; they'd gone into hiding and certainly weren't up for a fight.

There's one more possibility to consider. What if the disciples made it all up? What if they lied about the empty tomb and told stories about seeing Jesus alive, none of which were true? But why make up a story that if uncovered would make you look foolish and put your life in danger? Why invent a story which would have meant living with the guilt and dying for a lie? The threat of death is usually a good lie detector. There is no sane motive for them making this up. And if it was all a story, it doesn't explain how the disciples switched from being scared and in hiding to bold and telling everyone about Jesus.

Don't forget that the authorities could have put an end to all the rumours by producing the dead body of Jesus; they did not because they could not. And one more thing – Jesus was seen by more than five hundred people in the same place and at the same time; [9] mass hallucinations just don't happen.

The evidence speaks for itself. Jesus really died. Jesus really did rise from the dead. I'm not sure if you realize the significance of that yet, but consider this: if He did rise again, then Jesus has answered one of life's great questions and defeated life's greatest enemy. There really is life after death, and death can't be life's most powerful reality – Jesus is! It further proves that Jesus is God.

WHAT DOES TRUE CHRISTIANITY LOOK LIKE?

Seeing Jesus alive transformed the disciples completely. It would do, wouldn't it? It's like they came back to life too. But Jesus gave them something more than proof He was alive. He also promised them a new power [10] to help them begin and complete their new life as Christians (followers of Christ). Jesus told them to wait in Jerusalem[11] because there, God was going to fill these ordinary men with a powerful supernatural reality called His Holy Spirit (that's God's powerful, invisible presence actively living within them). More about this later in the chapter.

So they did just that; they waited in Jerusalem till they received what they had been promised. The following words record what happened when Peter, one of the disciples, told the people in Jerusalem the good news about the risen Jesus.

WHEN THE PEOPLE HEARD THIS, THEY WERE CUT TO THE HEART AND SAID TO PETER AND THE OTHER APOSTLES, 'BROTHERS, WHAT SHALL WE DO?' PETER REPLIED, 'REPENT AND BE BAPTISED, EVERY ONE OF YOU, IN THE NAME OF JESUS CHRIST FOR THE FORGIVENESS OF YOUR SINS. AND YOU WILL RECEIVE THE GIFT OF THE HOLY SPIRIT ... '
THOSE WHO ACCEPTED HIS MESSAGE WERE BAPTISED, AND ABOUT THREE THOUSAND WERE ADDED TO THEIR NUMBER THAT DAY.
Acts 2:37,38,41 (NIV)

Three thousand sounds a lot, but that was only the beginning of the spread of Christianity. Jerusalem was only the start; next it was the surrounding regions and eventually it reached the rest of the known world.

IT'S POWER TO MAKE A START

Can you remember what it felt like on your first day of senior school? Everything was new; everyone knew what they were doing and where they are going, except for you. That's what it felt like, anyway. Starting out as a Christian can feel much the same, but amazingly God has promised that every person who puts their faith in Jesus will also be given the same powerful reality He gave the disciples – the Holy Spirit.

Becoming a Christian is not like joining the gym, or a new club. It's much more exciting than that! Here's what happens: God sends His Holy Spirit to give you new life and make you new from the inside out; that's just what was about to happen to Peter's listeners.

BECOMING A CHRISTIAN IS NOT LIKE JOINING THE GYM, OR A NEW CLUB.

His message about Jesus hit them deep in the heart. With God's help it made sense to them; they were moved by it and wanted desperately to become Christians. But they weren't sure what to do, or what would happen next. Peter's response helped them, and will help us to understand as well.

Peter said 'Repent', which means to turn away from our sinful life and to turn to God. They also needed to stop believing what they used to believe and start believing what was true about Jesus. So, repent and believe – and the third thing is to be baptized (literally being dunked into water). Being baptized doesn't make you a Christian; it is possible to be a Christian without being baptized, but getting baptized shows your friends, family and everybody else in a powerful visual way that something special has happened to you. As you go down into the water and then back up again, it's symbolic – like the old you has died and there's a new one raised to life. You're different now! It says you are a Christian, but it doesn't make you a Christian – that's what the Holy Spirit does, not the water.

IT'S POWER TO MAKE PROGRESS

God's Holy Spirit gives us the power to make a fresh start, and it's the same power from God that helps every Christian to keep going all the way to heaven. You may be thinking. 'I could never keep it up', 'What would my friends say?', 'What if I mess it up?' These are very natural concerns to which God has given us a supernatural response – 'Never will I leave you'. [12] Think about it; if God's Spirit lives in us, then He's with us wherever we go and whatever we go through.

So God doesn't leave us to do this on our own – the Holy Spirit stays with us and helps every Christian in many different ways. God's Holy Spirit helps them to understand the Bible, gives them the power to change, the power to become more like Jesus, and the power to keep going to the end. He also reassures them that they are now part God's family. He helps them to see what is right and wrong; He leads and guides them in all their decision-making. God knows that you can't start or finish this without Him. That's why He has

GOD DOESN'T LEAVE US TO DO THIS ON OUR OWN – THE HOLY SPIRIT STAYS WITH US.

promised the Holy Spirit to help you make progress every day and every step of the way. [13]

IT'S POWER TO MAKE A DIFFERENCE

Before Jesus went back to heaven, He not only promised His disciples the power of His Holy Spirit, He also gave them a powerful new mission to fulfil. He said:

'. . . GO AND MAKE DISCIPLES OF ALL NATIONS, BAPTIZING THEM IN THE NAME OF THE FATHER AND OF THE SON AND OF THE HOLY SPIRIT, AND TEACHING THEM TO OBEY EVERYTHING I HAVE COMMANDED YOU. AND SURELY I AM WITH YOU ALWAYS . . .'
Matthew 28:19–20 (NIV)

In short: 'Go tell the nations about Me, and get them to do the same!'

Ever played the team game called British Bulldog? It's lots of fun and definitely competitive. The idea of the game is to get from one base to another without getting tagged. If you get tagged, then you change sides; you join the team of taggers. That's how Jesus wants His good news to spread. Disciples, or followers of Jesus, are to go and make disciples, who are to go and make disciples and so on. There should be no spectators in Christianity; everyone has a job to do [14] and a part to play – even you!

Who knows, then, what a difference YOU could make to this world as you respond with real faith and then begin to share with others the meaning of life and the truth about God?

THE END OR JUST THE BEGINNING?

This may be the end of the book, but for you it could also be the beginning of a brilliant new life and a completely different direction. If you have put your faith in Jesus, then here are a few things to help you on your way:

A RELATIONSHIP TO ENJOY

The best way to get to know a new friend is to spend time with them; that means both listening and talking. We get to know God better as we spend time reading the Bible and praying.

You don't have to use special words or sentences when you pray; you can just talk to God. You can pray any time or anywhere. God loves to hear the prayers of new Christians.

A BOOK TO READ

The Bible is an amazing book written with God's powerful influence. In the Bible, God has told you everything you need to know about life on earth and the life to come. He's told you everything you need to know about yourself and about Himself. You may find it helpful to choose a time every day when you can read a little bit more of the Bible and pray. Reading through one of the Gospels (Matthew, Mark, Luke or John) would be a great place to start.

A CHURCH TO JOIN

Not every church is the same. You need to find a church with people who love Jesus, who believe the Bible is true, who are serious about obeying God, and passionate in sharing the good news about Jesus with others. If you are struggling to find the right church, then the Changing Lanes website contains some more advice – www.changinglanes.org.uk

A JOB TO DO

God saves people on purpose and for a purpose. He has planned a special role for every Christian to carry out. It may take a little bit of time for you to work out what that plan is – for some it might be volunteering, for others it might even become a full-time role – but through prayer, reading the Bible and attending a good church you should be able to discover God's purpose for you.

A MISSION TO FULFIL

Every Christian is to be involved in God's exciting worldwide mission to share the good news about Jesus with the nations. It's great that you are now on the narrow road that leads to life, but what about those still on the other road? Jesus wants every Christian to get involved in His rescue plan for people. There are loads of ways you can do that; why not start by asking God who He wants you to share your rescue story with?

A JOURNEY TO COMPLETE

Life on the narrow road is exciting but not easy; you'll have some difficult times ahead, but don't turn back, however tough it gets. God has promised to be with you all the way and to give you everything you need for the journey.

REFERENCES

Many of the following references are from the Bible. If you don't have a copy, you can order one from the Changing Lanes Store (www.changinglanes.org.uk). As I explained in chapter 5, the Bible contains sixty-six books in total and is split into two big sections called Testaments. Each of the sixty-six books is split up into chapters like any other book. The chapters are then split up again into short sentences called verses. Chapters usually have bigger numbers and verses smaller numbers. If you ever have trouble finding what you are looking for, then use the contents page at the front of the Bible.

CHAPTER 1

1. John 14:6 (NIV).

2. To read more about the God revealed in the Bible, see Help / FAQs section www.changinglanes.org.uk

CHAPTER 2

1. See http://www.answersingenesis.org/home/area/bios/

2. Illustration taken from Andrew Christofides, *Evidences for God: Seven Reasons to Believe in the Existence of God* (Leominster: Day One Publications, 2010), p.13.

3. Adam Goddard, Bournemouth.

4. Luke 19:1–10.

CHAPTER 3

1. NASA – National Aeronautics and Space Administration.

2. Matthew 7:13 (NIV).

3. Romans 3:23 (NIV).

CHAPTER 4

1. Mark 2:11 (NIV).

2. Mark 4:39 (NIV).

3. Luke 8:54 (NIV).

4. See for example Mark 8:31.

5. Matthew 25:41–46; Mark 9:42–48 (NIV).

6. Mark 9:43.

CHAPTER 5

1. Micah 5:2.

2. Psalm 22; Isaiah 53.

3. Luke 2:46,47.

4. Matthew 7:28,29.

5. Luke 13:17.

6. Mark 1:27,28.

7. Matthew 20:34.

8. Mark 7:37.

9. John 5:7,8.

10. John 4:50–54.

11. Luke 8:43–48.

12. Mark 5:35–43; Luke 7:11–17; John 11:38–44.

13. John 2:1–11.

14. 2 Peter 1:16.

15. Flavius Josephus, *Jewish Antiquities 18:63*.

16. Cornelius Tacitus, *Annuls 15:44*.

17. Idea taken from chapter 3 of *Mere Christianity* by
C.S. Lewis (London: HarperCollins, 1997).

18. See for example Luke 6:27–36; see also John 13:34,35;
Luke 23:34.

19. Mark 4:40 (NIV).

CHAPTER 6

1. Matthew 1:21.

2. John 19:4–6 (NKJV).

3. John 19:19.

4. Romans 6:23 (NIV).

5. To read more about the God revealed in the Bible, see
Help / FAQs section www.changinglanes.org.uk

6. Mark 8:31.

7. Matthew 26:59,60.

8. Luke 23:18–21 (NIV).

9. Luke 22:4–6.

10. Mark 14:50.

11. John 19:16.

12. Matthew 27:27–31.

13. Mark 15:34 (NIV).

14. Isaiah 53:4–6; 2 Corinthians 5:21.

15. John 19:30 (NIV).

16. Romans 6:23 (NIV), my italics.

CHAPTER 7

1. John 20:19.

2. Read more in *The Resurrection Factor* by Josh McDowell (Milton Keynes: Authentic Media, 2005).

3. John 19:34,35.

4. Matthew 27:57–60.

5. Matthew 27:61.

6. Matthew 28:1–3.

7. Matthew 27:60.

8. Matthew 27:65,66.

9. 1 Corinthians 15:6.

10. Acts 1:8.

11. Acts 1:4.

12. Hebrews 13:5 (NIV).

13. Acts 1:4–8.

14. Ephesians 2:10.